LONGMAN CLASSICS

Oliver Twist

Charles Dickens

Simplified by Margaret Maison,
D K Swan and Michael West

Longman Group UK Limited,
Longman House, Burnt Mill, Harlow,
Essex CM20 2JE, England
and Associated Companies throughout the world.

First published 1987

ISBN 0-582-52279-X

Set in 10/13 point Linotron 202 Versailles
Produced by Longman Group (FE) Limited
Printed in Hong Kong

Acknowledgements

The photographs are from the film OLIVER TWIST © Southbrook International Programmes Ltd.

The cover background is a wallpaper design called NUAGE, courtesy of Osborne and Little plc.

Stage 4: 1800 word vocabulary

Contents

Introduction

Charles Dickens
Charles Dickens, born in 1812, was the son of a clerk in a government office. His father spent more money than he earned, and Charles Dickens was still a boy when his father was sent to prison for debt. In those days, men who owed quite small amounts had to stay in prison until the debt was paid.

One result was that Charles's education was interrupted. Another result was that he had experience of the unhappy life of many poor people, including children. In years of hard work in various unpleasant jobs, he met large numbers of people, young and old, rich and poor, happy and miserable. He had unusual energy and unusual powers of observation. He worked hard to improve his knowledge and at the same time he stored away memories of all the people he met – the men he worked for, the boys he worked with, the London scenes and London characters.

He learnt to write shorthand, and he became a newspaper reporter, using his shorthand to record speeches and conversations in different parts of England and finally in Parliament.

He began to write sketches – short stories and descriptions – for weekly and monthly magazines. Readers enjoyed these sketches, especially those which showed Dickens's humour, his rich sense of fun. The *Pickwick Papers* appeared in parts in 1836–37, and the public loved them. Mr Pickwick is the very simple, innocent observer of the behaviour of the people of his time. He is shocked by the wickedness he finds. Sam Weller, his servant, is a worldly-wise, clever fellow who gets Mr Pickwick out of trouble with all the humour of the London "Cockney".

The *Pickwick Papers* were immediately popular, and Dickens was soon in a position to make the writing of novels his one profession. The stories poured from his pen. They all appeared in weekly or monthly parts before being collected in books. Here are the most important of them in the order of writing, with the date of appearance as a book:

1838 *Oliver Twist*; 1839 *Nicholas Nickleby*;

1841 *The Old Curiosity Shop*; 1848 *Dombey and Son*;

1849 *David Copperfield*; 1850 *Hard Times*;

1859 *A Tale of Two Cities*; 1861 *Great Expectations*.

Dickens's characters were much better or much worse than they would be in real life. They were exaggerated in rather the same way as artists exaggerate in their drawings of political and other leaders in newspaper cartoons today. But the readers of Dickens's time accepted such exaggeration. They were perhaps readier to laugh or cry over the novelist's characters and situations than we are today.

The novels of Dickens are full of life, observation and energy, and his own energy seemed endless. His books were popular in the English-speaking countries on both sides of the Atlantic. In later years he travelled widely in Britain and America, reading from his books to eager audiences. His sudden death in 1870 shocked thousands of people who were waiting for his next book. Instead, they bought, and wept over, a picture called "The Empty Chair", showing the desk and chair that he would no longer use.

Oliver Twist

Dickens wrote *Oliver Twist* in the years 1837–38. The dates are important. In 1834 Parliament passed a new Poor Law. This law was based on the idea that there was work for everybody, and that if a person had no work and no money, it was because he or she was lazy and did not want to work. For such people the local government provided a workhouse, with beds and food, but it must not be comfortable or (the idea was) people might want to stay there instead of looking for work. So the workhouses were unfriendly places – inhuman, Dickens thought – where nobody would want to remain if he or she could find work. The people who controlled them were sometimes unfeeling men almost like Mr Bumble in *Oliver Twist*.

Another Act of Parliament that was beginning to have an effect was the Metropolitan Police Act of 1829. That Act set up a police force for the capital. By the time Dickens was writing *Oliver Twist*, the police had become effective enough to make it hard for a murderer like Bill Sikes to escape. They were not yet able to put an end to all the crime that is represented in this book by Fagin and his gang of boy thieves.

It was a time of cruel punishments if a criminal was caught. That is why, in the story, the evil Monks wants Fagin to turn Oliver into a thief. Even a boy of Oliver's age could be hanged for a serious crime.

It was a time when national and local governments did little to help those people who were old, ill, or badly treated by employers and others. But there were also kind people like Mr Brownlow, Mrs Maylie and Rose, who were ready to help those who were less fortunate than themselves.

Chapter 1
Oliver asks for more

Among other buildings in a town in England, there was a house for poor people. They went there when they had no money and nowhere to live. It was called the workhouse.

Oliver Twist was born in the workhouse. His mother, a young woman, lay ill in bed. A doctor and an old woman stood by her side.

"Let me see the child and die," the young woman said.

"Oh, you must not talk about dying yet," said the doctor.

"No, dear," said the old woman. "You are too young to die."

The young woman shook her head and held out her hand towards the child.

The doctor put the child in her arms. She pressed her cold white lips to its face, and then fell back – and died.

"She's dead," said the doctor.

"Yes, poor dear," said the old woman, as she took the child away from its dead mother. "Poor dear."

"She was a good-looking girl," said the doctor, as he put on his hat and gloves. "Where did she come from?"

"She was brought here last night," said the old woman. "She was lying in the street. She had walked a long way and her shoes were worn out. Nobody knows where she came from, or where she was going to."

The doctor raised the dead woman's left hand.

"The old story," he said. "I see that she has no ring on her finger! She was not married. Good night!"

He went home to his dinner. The old woman sat down on a chair in front of the fire and began to dress the baby.

She dressed him in the very old clothes used for a baby born in the workhouse – a poor child without father or mother, born into a world which had no love or pity for him.

From the age of nine, Oliver had to work. He had only three meals of soup every day. The soup was very thin. It was made by boiling very little meat and some roots in a lot of water. He had a small piece of bread on Sundays.

The room in which the boys were fed was a big hall. A large pot stood at one end. When it was time for meals, a master served the soup from the pot to the boys.

Each boy had one small bowl of soup and no more. The bowls never needed washing. The boys cleaned them with their spoons until they shone.

Oliver Twist and his friends grew so wild with hunger that they decided to choose a boy to walk up to the master after supper and ask for more. They boy chosen was Oliver Twist.

The evening arrived, and the boys took their places. The master stood by the pot, and the soup was served.

It disappeared quickly. The boys whispered and made signs to Oliver.

He rose from the table and went to the master.

"Please, sir," he said, "I want some more."

The master looked with surprise at the small boy.

"What?" said the master at last in a faint voice.

"Please, sir," said Oliver, "I want some more."

The master hit Oliver with his spoon, then seized him in his arms and cried for help. Mr Bumble came rushing into the room. Mr Bumble was an important officer in the town. The master told him what Oliver had said.

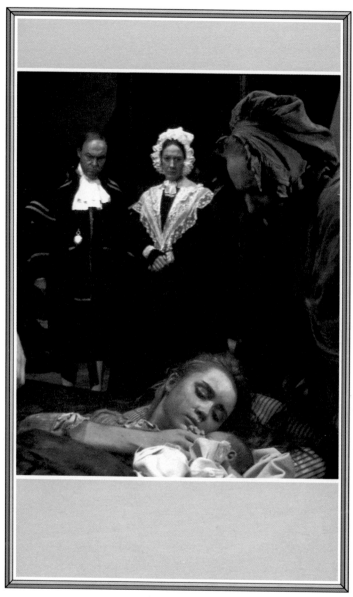

Oliver Twist is born

Oliver asks for more

"He asked for more?" Mr Bumble cried. "I can hardly believe it. That boy will live to be hanged!"

He took Oliver away and shut him up in a dark room. The next morning a notice appeared on the gate of the workhouse. This notice offered five pounds to anybody who would take Oliver Twist.

Oliver was a prisoner in that dark room for a whole week. The weather was cold. Every morning he was taken to wash in the yard, and Mr Bumble beat him with a stick. Then he was taken into the hall where the boys had their soup, and Mr Bumble beat him in front of everybody. He cried all day and could not sleep at night.

But one day outside the workhouse gate, Mr Bumble met Mr Sowerberry. Mr Sowerberry was a tall thin man who made coffins for dead bodies. Many of his coffins were for the poor people who died in the workhouse.

"I have prepared the coffins for the two women who died last night," said Mr Sowerberry to Mr Bumble.

"Good," said Mr Bumble. "By the way, you don't know anybody who wants a boy, do you? And five pounds." He raised his stick and pointed to the notice on the gate.

Chapter 2
He goes out to work

It was soon arranged for Oliver to start work with Mr Sowerberry. Mr Bumble took him to the shop that evening.

Mr Sowerberry had closed the shop, and he was writing by the light of a candle.

"Here, Mr Sowerberry, I've brought the boy," said Mr Bumble.

Oliver bowed.

"Oh, that's the boy, is it?" said Mr Sowerberry, raising the candle above his head to get a better view of Oliver. "Mrs Sowerberry, come here, my dear."

A short thin woman with a face like a fox came out from a little room behind the shop.

"My dear," said Mr Sowerberry, "this is the boy from the workhouse that I told you about."

Oliver bowed again.

"Oh!" said the woman. "He's very small."

"Yes, he *is* rather small!" said Mr Bumble, looking at Oliver as if it were the boy's fault that he was no bigger. "He *is* small. That's true. But he'll grow, Mrs Sowerberry, he'll grow."

"Yes, I expect he will," said the lady angrily, "on *our* food and *our* drink. These children cost a lot of money to keep. Here, get downstairs, you little bag of bones. You can have some of those bits of cold meat which we'd saved for the dog. The dog hasn't come home since this morning, so it won't have them."

Oliver's eyes shone at the thought of meat. They gave him a plate of the dog's food. He ate it all very quickly.

Mrs Sowerberry watched him. She was not pleased to see how eager he was to eat.

"Come with me," she said, taking a dirty lamp and leading the way upstairs. "Your bed is in the shop. You don't mind sleeping among the coffins, I suppose? But it doesn't much matter whether you do or you don't, for you can't sleep anywhere else. Come along. Don't keep me here all night."

Oliver was afraid all night.

The next morning he heard a loud knocking noise outside the shop door.

"Open the door, will you?" cried a voice.

"I will at once, sir," replied Oliver, turning the key.

Oliver opened the door. He saw nobody but a big boy sitting in front of the house, eating bread and butter. He had small eyes and a red nose.

"Did you knock?" asked Oliver.

"I did."

"Did you want a coffin?" said Oliver.

"You don't know who I am, I suppose, Workhouse?" said the boy.

"No, sir," replied Oliver.

"I'm *Mr* Noah Claypole," said the boy, "and you will work under me. Open the windows at once!"

Noah was a poor boy, but not from the workhouse. He knew who his parents were – his mother washed clothes and his father was a drunken soldier. Other boys were rude to him, so he was glad that Oliver had come because now he in turn could be rude to Oliver.

Chapter 3
He runs away

During the months which followed, Noah Claypole made life very unpleasant for Oliver. Because Mr Sowerberry tried to be his friend, Mrs Sowerberry was his enemy. Oliver's life was not comfortable.

One day Noah was very bad to Oliver. He pulled his hair hard and hurt his ears. He was trying to make Oliver cry.

"How's your mother, Workhouse?" he said.

"She's dead," replied Oliver. "Don't you say anything about her to me."

"What!" cried Noah. "Don't be rude, Workhouse. We all pity you, Workhouse, but your mother was a bad woman. You know she was!"

"What did you say?" asked Oliver, looking up quickly.

"A bad woman, Workhouse," repeated Noah.

Red with anger, Oliver pushed over the chair and table, seized the much bigger boy by the neck, shook him and then threw him to the ground.

"He'll murder me!" cried Noah. "Help, Mrs Sowerberry! Oliver has gone mad!"

Mrs Sowerberry came rushing into the kitchen. She held Oliver and scratched his face. Noah got up and hit him from behind. When they were tired and could tear and scratch and beat no longer, they carried Oliver to a dark room and shut him in there.

Mrs Sowerberry sat down and began to cry. "We might all have been murdered in our beds," she said. "But what shall we do? Mr Sowerberry is not at home. There's no man in the house. Run to Mr Bumble,

Noah, and tell him to come here at once."

Noah found Mr Bumble at the workhouse.

"Oh, Mr Bumble, sir!" cried Noah "Oliver, sir, Oliver has——"

"What? What?" asked Mr Bumble with a look of pleasure in his eyes. "Not run away, he hasn't run away, has he, Noah?"

"Not run away, sir, but he attacked me and tried to murder me, sir. And then he tried to murder Mrs Sowerberry, sir. Oh, the terrible pain!" And Noah moved his body as if still suffering from Oliver's attack.

"My poor boy," said Mr Bumble. "I'll come at once."

He took his stick and set off with Noah to Mr Sowerberry's shop. He went to the dark room and said in a deep voice:

"Oliver!"

"Let me out!" cried Oliver from the inside.

"Do you know this voice, Oliver?" asked Mr Bumble.

"Yes," answered Oliver.

"Aren't you afraid of it? Have you no fear while I speak?"

"No!" said Oliver in a courageous voice.

This answer was so different from the one he expected to receive, Mr Bumble was very surprised. He stood back from the door and looked at the others.

"Oh, you know, Mr Bumble, he must be mad," said Mrs Sowerberry. "No good boy could speak to you like that."

"He is not mad," said Mr Bumble after a few moments' deep thought. "The trouble is – Meat!"

"What?" said Mrs Sowerberry.

"Meat, Mrs Sowerberry, meat," said Mr Bumble. "You have given him too much to eat. If you had fed him only on

Mr Bumble

soup, as we did in the workhouse, this would never have happened."

"Dear, dear!" said Mrs Sowerberry. "This is the result of being generous."

"Leave him in there for a day or two," said Mr Bumble. "Give him nothing but soup in future, Mrs Sowerberry. He comes of a bad family."

At this moment Mr Sowerberry arrived. He wanted to be kind to Oliver, but when his wife began to cry he felt forced to beat Oliver. He hit him hard and then shut him up in the dark room again. At night Oliver was ordered upstairs to his bed in the shop.

It was not until he was left alone in the silence of the shop that Oliver began to cry. He fell on his knees on the floor and, hiding his face in his hands, he wept.

For a long time he stayed like that, without moving. Then he opened the door and looked out. It was a cold, dark night. He shut the door, tied up his few clothes in a handkerchief, and sat down to wait for morning.

When the first light of day showed through the windows he opened the door. After one quick frightened look around him he closed the door behind him and was out in the open street.

Chapter 4
London

Oliver looked to the right and to the left, not knowing where to go. He remembered seeing the carts, as they left the town, going up the hill. He took the same road.

He ran, afraid that he might be followed and caught. At last he sat down by a milestone. The milestone showed that it was just seventy miles to London. London! That great big place! Nobody, not even Mr Bumble, could find him there.

He had a piece of dry bread, an old shirt and two pairs of socks. He had a penny too.

"But these will not help me to walk seventy miles in the winter time," he thought.

He walked twenty miles that day. All the time he ate nothing but the piece of dry bread and had a few drinks of water. When night came, he slept in a field. He was frightened at first, and very cold and hungry. But he was very tired, and he soon fell asleep and forgot his troubles.

Next morning he was cold, and he was so hungry that he had to spend his penny on bread. He walked only twelve miles that day. Another night in the cold air made him worse. His feet hurt and his legs felt weak. He could hardly walk.

As the days passed, he grew weaker. A man gave him a meal of bread and cheese, and an old lady gave him food and some kind words. Without this, he would have fallen dead on the road.

Early on the seventh morning Oliver walked slowly into the little town of Barnet, a few miles from London. The streets were empty. Oliver sat on a doorstep. He was covered in dust, and there was blood on his feet.

People began to pass, but no one spoke to him. Then he saw a boy looking at him. The boy walked up to Oliver. "Hello! What's the trouble?"

He was a strange boy. He was about Oliver's age but he behaved like a man. He wore a man's coat, which reached nearly to his feet, and a man's hat, which looked as if it would fall off at any moment.

"What is it?" he asked Oliver.

"I am very hungry and tired," said Oliver. "I have been walking for seven days." The tears rose to his eyes.

"Seven days!" said the boy. "Oh, I see! You need food. I'll pay for you. Up you get!"

He helped Oliver to rise and took him to an inn where Oliver had a good meal with his new friend.

"Going to London?" said the strange boy, when Oliver had at last finished.

"Yes."

"Have you got anywhere to stay?"

"No. Do you live in London?" said Oliver.

"Yes, I do, when I'm at home. I suppose you want somewhere to sleep tonight, don't you?"

"Yes," answered Oliver.

"Don't trouble yourself any more about it," said the boy. "I'm going to London tonight, and I know an old gentleman who will give you a bed for nothing. He knows me very well."

Oliver found that the boy's name was Jack Dawkins. Jack refused to enter London before dark, so it was nearly eleven o'clock before they reached the city. He walked fast and Oliver followed him down a narrow street into one of the dirtiest places he had ever seen.

Oliver began to think that he ought to run away, but suddenly Dawkins caught him by the arm, pushed open the door of a house and pulled him inside.

Dawkins took Oliver's hand and helped him up the dark and broken stairs. He threw open the door of a room and drew Oliver in after him.

The walls of the room were completely black with age and dirt. Some meat was cooking over the fire.

There was a very old man standing by the fire. His name was Fagin. He was dressed in dirty clothes and his evil-looking face was half hidden by his red hair. He seemed to be dividing his attention between the meat and a line on which a lot of silk handkerchiefs were hanging. Several rough beds were placed side by side on the floor. Four or five boys were sitting round the table. They were smoking long pipes like men.

"This is Oliver Twist," said Jack Dawkins.

The old man took Oliver by the hand and said that he hoped to have the honour of his friendship. Then the young men with the pipes came round and shook both Oliver's hands very hard, especially the hand in which he held his handkerchief. One young man was anxious to hang up his cap for him and another put his hands in Oliver's pockets to save Oliver the trouble of emptying them before he went to bed.

"We are very glad to see you, Oliver," said Fagin. "Ah, you're looking at all those pocket handkerchiefs. We've just got them ready to wash. That's all, Oliver, that's all. Ha! ha! ha!"

The boys all laughed at this, and they began to have their supper. Oliver ate with them. Then they gave him a bed on the floor and he fell into a deep sleep.

Jack Dawkins

Chapter 5
Fagin

It was late next morning when Oliver awoke from a long sleep. There was nobody in the room but the old man.

Fagin thought that Oliver was still asleep. He locked the door and then he drew out a box from a secret hole in the floor. He placed the box carefully on the table. He then sat down and took from the box a splendid gold watch, bright with jewels.

He took out at least six more watches. He looked at them with pleasure. There were also some beautiful rings and other splendid jewels in the box.

Suddenly he looked up at Oliver's face. The boy's eyes were fixed on his in silent curiosity. Fagin knew that Oliver had seen what he was doing. He shut the box quickly, took a bread knife from the table and went over to Oliver.

"Why are you awake? What have you seen? Speak out, boy! Quick – quick! For your life!"

"I wasn't able to sleep any longer, sir," said Oliver. "I am very sorry if I have troubled you. I have only just woken up."

"Did you see any of these pretty things?" said Fagin.

"Yes, sir."

"Ah!" said Fagin, putting down the knife. "They're mine, Oliver. All I have to live on in my old age."

At that moment Jack Dawkins came in, with another boy called Charley Bates.

"Well, my dears," said Fagin, "I hope you've been at work this morning. What have *you* got, Dawkins?"

"Two purses," said Dawkins, and he gave them to

Fagin, who looked at them.

"Not very heavy," said the old m...
He's good at his work, isn't he, Oliver?

"Very good," said Oliver.

"And what have you got?" said Fagin to C...

"Handkerchiefs," replied Master Bates, producin...

"Well," said Fagin, looking at them carefully. "Th...
good ones but they are marked, Charley. So the mar...
must be taken out with a needle and we'll teach Oliver how
to do it. Shall we, Oliver? Ha! ha! ha!"

"If you please, sir," said Oliver.

After breakfast the old gentleman and the two boys
played a very strange game. The old man placed a silver
box in one pocket of his trousers, a purse in the other, and
a watch and a handkerchief in his coat pocket.

He then walked round and round the room with a stick,
just as old gentlemen walk in the streets. Sometimes he
stopped at the door, pretending to look at a shop window.
Then he looked round, for fear of thieves. He kept
touching his pockets to see if he had lost something. He
did this in such a funny way that Oliver laughed till the
tears came to his eyes.

All this time the two boys followed close behind Fagin.
They got out of his sight very quickly when he turned
round. At last Dawkins stepped on Fagin's foot, while
Charley Bates pushed against him from behind. In that
one moment they quickly took from him the silver box,
purse, watch and handkerchief. If the old gentleman felt a
hand in any one of his pockets he cried out where it was,
and then the game began all over again.

They played this game a great many times, but it ended
when two young ladies came in. One of them was called

an, "but well made.

harley.
g four.
ey're
s

with Dawkins and

ed Oliver.
l some work to do
hanging out of my

my feeling it, as you
this morning."
ocket with one hand,
d it, and drew the

"Is it gone?

"Here it is, sir," said Oliver, showing it in his hand.

"You're a good boy, my dear," said Fagin. "And now come here, and I'll show you how to take the marks out of the handkerchiefs."

Oliver could not understand how this game could help him to become a great man, but he was not yet ten years old, and thought that Fagin, being so much older, must know best.

Chapter 6
Oliver among the thieves

Day after day Oliver stayed in Fagin's room, taking the marks out of the handkerchiefs. Sometimes too he played the game already described. At last he began to want fresh air and he begged Fagin to let him go out to work with Dawkins and Charley Bates.

One morning Fagin allowed him to go. The three boys set out, walking very slowly. Oliver wondered if they were going to work at all.

Suddenly Dawkins stopped. Laying his finger on his lips, he drew his friends back with great care.

"Quiet!" he said. "Do you see that old man near the bookshop? He'll do."

"Perfect," said Charley Bates.

Oliver looked at them in surprise. The two boys walked across the road and came close behind the old gentleman. Oliver followed them, not knowing what to do.

The old gentleman had white hair and gold glasses. He wore a green coat and carried a stick. He had taken a book from a shelf in front of the shop and he stood reading it.

To Oliver's surprise, Dawkins put his hand into the old man's pocket and took out a handkerchief. He gave it to Charley Bates and they both ran away quickly.

At once Oliver understood the mystery of the handkerchiefs and the watches and the jewels and Fagin's games. He stood still for a moment, full of fear, and then he too began to run.

At that moment the old gentleman put his hand in his pocket and, not finding his handkerchief, turned round. He saw Oliver running away and thought of course that the boy had stolen his handkerchief.

"Stop, thief!" he shouted, and ran after Oliver.

Everybody in the street joined him in the pursuit. "Stop, thief!" they cried. Even Dawkins and Charley Bates, when they heard the cry, began to shout "Stop, thief!" and run after Oliver too.

At last someone hit Oliver and he fell to the ground, covered with dust. There was blood all over his face. A crowd collected.

"Is this the boy?" they asked the old gentleman.

"Yes," said the old gentleman, "I'm afraid it is. Poor boy! He's hurt."

A constable made his way through the crowd and seized Oliver by the neck.

"Get up!" he said.

"It wasn't me, sir. It was two other boys," said Oliver. "They are here somewhere."

"Oh, no, they're not," said the officer.

"Don't hurt him," said the old gentleman.

The constable began to pull Oliver along the street. Suddenly a man, dressed in an old black suit, came towards them.

"Stop, stop! Don't take him away!" he cried. "Stop a moment!"

"What is this? Who are you?" said the constable.

"I own the bookshop," replied the man, "and I saw what happened. There were three boys – two others and this one. Mr Brownlow was reading and another boy took his handkerchief. This boy did nothing. He stood still and ~oked surprised."

'Then the boy must go free," said the constable. He let ~liver's neck and at once the boy fell down in a faint.

boy, poor boy!" said Mr Brownlow, the old

gentleman. "Call a carriage, somebody, please. At once!"

A carriage came. Oliver was placed on one of the seats. The old gentleman got in and sat beside him.

They rode away until the carriage stopped in front of a pleasant house in a quiet London street. Oliver was taken into the house and put to bed.

When Dawkins and Charley Bates got home, Fagin was waiting for them.

"Where's Oliver?" he said with an angry look.

The young thieves looked at him and then at each other, but they said nothing.

"What's happened to that boy?" cried Fagin, seizing Dawkins. "Speak out or I'll kill you!"

"A constable took him away," answered Dawkins. "Let go of me!"

He broke free and took a knife from the table. Fagin picked up a cup and threw it at Dawkins's head. It missed him and nearly hit a man who was entering the room at that moment.

"Who threw that at me?" said the man in a deep voice. He was a strong fellow of about thirty-five, with dirty clothes and angry eyes. His name was Bill Sikes. A white dog, with its face scratched and torn in twenty different places, followed him into the room.

"What are you doing to those boys, Fagin?" said Bill Sikes. "I'm surprised they don't murder you."

"Quiet, Mr Sikes," said Fagin. "Don't speak so loud. You seem angry today."

"Perhaps I am," said Bill Sikes. "Give me a drink, Fagin."

While Sikes was drinking, Dawkins told them about Oliver and how he had been caught.

"I'm afraid," said Fagin, "that the boy may tell the constable all about us and get us into trouble. We must find him."

The door opened and the two young ladies, Bet and Nancy, came in.

"Ah!" said Fagin. "Bet will go, won't you, my dear?"

"Where?" said Bet.

"To the police station – to find where Oliver is. He's been taken away and we must get him back."

"No!" said Bet.

"Nancy, my dear," said Fagin. "What do you say?"

"No," said Nancy.

"She'll go, Fagin," said Sikes. He looked very angry.

At last Nancy agreed to go to look for Oliver. She put on clean clothes and carried a little basket. She looked very good and sweet.

"Oh, my brother, Oliver! My poor dear little brother, Oliver!" cried Nancy, pretending to weep. "What has happened to him? Where have they taken him? Oh, do have pity and tell me what's been done with the dear boy!"

"Very good!" said Fagin and Bill Sikes. "You're a fine girl, Nancy. Go and see the constable now."

When Nancy returned, she told them what had happened to Oliver.

"A gentleman has got him," she said. "A gentleman called Mr Brownlow – the man whose handkerchief Dawkins took. But they don't know where he lives."

"He must be found!" cried Fagin. "Charley, you must watch that bookshop every day. We must find Oliver. I shall shut up this house at once. It's no longer safe here. You know where to find me. Don't stop here a minute longer, my dears. And find Oliver. Find him, I say!"

Bill Sikes

Chapter 7
A better home

Oliver stayed in Mr Brownlow's house. He was ill and he lay in bed for several weeks. When he was a little better, he was able to sit in a chair and talk to Mrs Bedwin, an old lady who looked after the house for Mr Brownlow.

His new friends were very kind to him. Mr Brownlow gave him new clothes and a new pair of shoes. Mrs Bedwin fed him with good food.

One day he sat in Mrs Bedwin's room, and he noticed a picture on the wall. It was the picture of a lady. He stared at it.

"Are you fond of pictures, dear?" said Mrs Bedwin.

"I don't quite know," said Oliver. "I have seen so few that I hardly know. What a beautiful face that lady has! But the eyes look so sad and, wherever I sit, they seem fixed upon me."

"Oh!" cried the old lady. "Don't talk in that way, child. You're weak after your illness. Let me move your chair round to the other side and then you won't see it."

Then Mr Brownlow came down to see him. As they were talking Mr Brownlow looked at the picture.

"Mrs Bedwin!" he cried suddenly. "Look there!" As he spoke he pointed to the picture above Oliver's head and then to the boy's face. The eyes, the head, the mouth – they were the same. Each line of the living face seemed to be just like the other in the picture.

The next day, when Oliver came down to Mrs Bedwin's room for breakfast, the picture was gone.

"Why have they taken it away?" he asked.

"It seemed to trouble you, child," said Mrs Bedwin.

"Oh, no, indeed, it didn't trouble me," said Oliver. "I liked to see it. I quite loved it."

"Well, well," said the old lady. "You must get well as fast as you can, dear, and we'll hang it up again."

Oliver soon grew strong and well. He was very happy in Mr Brownlow's house. One day Mr Brownlow asked him what he wanted to do in the future.

"Please let me stay with you, sir," Oliver said. "Please don't send me away. Let me stay and be a servant in your house."

"You can stay," said Mr Brownlow, "and I'll never send you away unless you give me cause. But let me hear your story, Oliver. Where did you come from? Who looked after you when you were small?"

Oliver began to cry, and then he started to tell Mr Brownlow all about Mr Bumble and the workhouse. Just then a knock was heard on the door. It was Mr Grimwig, a friend of Mr Brownlow. He had come to tea.

"Shall I go, sir?" said Oliver.

"No, stay here," said Mr Brownlow. "This is young Oliver Twist, the boy I told you about," he said to Mr Grimwig. Oliver bowed.

Mr Grimwig looked at Oliver. He knew that his friend Mr Brownlow was very kind, and he was afraid that a boy found in the street might deceive him.

"So that's the boy, is it?" he said. "And where does he come from? Who is he? What is he? When are we going to hear?"

"Tomorrow morning," said Mr Brownlow. "Come up to me tomorrow at ten o'clock, Oliver, and we will talk about it all."

"Yes, sir."

Mr Grimwig whispered to Mr Brownlow. "You trust people too easily. That boy is deceiving you, my good friend."

"He is not," said Mr Brownlow.

"If he is not," said Mr Grimwig, "I'll eat my head!"

At that moment, Mrs Bedwin came in with some books.

"These books must go back to the shop this evening, sir," she said.

"Send Oliver with them," said Mr Grimwig. "If you can trust him, as you say, he will take the books back for you."

"Yes, do let me take them, if you please, sir," said Oliver. "I'll run all the way, sir."

Mr Brownlow did not really want Oliver to go, but he did want to show that Oliver could be trusted.

"Yes," he said to Oliver. "Tell the man at the bookshop that you have brought these books back, and that you have come to pay the four pounds I owe him. Here is a five pound note. You must bring me back a pound."

"I won't be long, sir," replied Oliver in an eager voice. He put the money in his pocket and the books under his arm, bowed and left the room.

"He'll be back in twenty minutes," said Mr Brownlow.

"Oh, you really expect him to come back, do you?" said Mr Grimwig.

"Don't you?" said Mr Brownlow, smiling.

"No," said Mr Grimwig. "I do not. That boy has new clothes on, good books under his arm and a five pound note in his pocket. He'll join his old friends the thieves, and laugh at you. If ever that boy returns to this house, I'll eat my head!"

Chapter 8
Back among the thieves

Oliver walked along until he came near the bookshop. Suddenly he heard a young woman shouting out in a loud voice, "Oh, my dear brother!"

He felt a pair of arms thrown round his neck.

"Let go of me!" he cried. "Who is it? Why are you stopping me?"

"I've found him!" cried the young woman. "Oh, Oliver! Oliver! Oh, you bad boy, to make me suffer so much!"

"What's this?" cried Bill Sikes, coming out of a shop with his white dog following him. "Young Oliver! Come home to your poor mother, you young fool. Come home at once."

Oliver was too weak to fight. What could one poor child do against all this? He was pulled along the narrow streets.

Night fell. At Mr Brownlow's house Mrs Bedwin stood at the open door. And the two old gentlemen sat upstairs, waiting in silence.

Nancy and Bill Sikes ran through the streets with Oliver. After half an hour they came to a very dirty narrow street.

Sikes rang a bell, the door opened, and all three quickly went inside the house. It was dark inside. Sikes pulled Oliver down the stairs and opened the door of a room.

Fagin bowed to Oliver.

"I am glad to see you," he said. "And you are looking so well. Charley will give you another suit, my dear – you must not spoil that Sunday suit."

At that moment Charley drew out Mr Brownlow's five

pound note from Oliver's pocket.

"Hello! What's that?" said Sikes, stepping forward as Fagin seized the note. "That's mine, Fagin."

"No, no, my dear," said Fagin. "Mine, Bill, mine. You can have the books."

"If that money isn't mine I'll take the boy back," said Sikes. "Nancy and I got the boy for you. Give us that money, you old devil."

With these words he took the note from Fagin's fingers.

"That's for our work," he said. "You may keep the books."

"They belong to the old gentleman," said Oliver, falling on his knees at Fagin's feet. "They belong to the good kind old gentleman who took me to his house and looked after me when I was so ill. Please send them back. Send him back the books and the money. He'll think I stole them, and the old lady will think so too. And they were so kind to me. Oh, please send them back!"

"The boy's right," said Fagin. "They will think you have stolen them. Ha, ha!" He laughed and rubbed his hands together. "It couldn't have happened better!"

Oliver now understood what had happened; he jumped quickly to his feet and, shouting for help at the top of his voice, he ran from the room. Fagin and the other boys rushed after him and soon brought him back.

"So you wanted to get away, my dear, did you?" said Fagin, taking up a stick. "You wanted to get help, did you? You meant to send for the police perhaps? We'll soon stop that."

He hit Oliver hard. He was raising the stick for a second blow when Nancy rushed forward, pulled the stick from his hand and threw it into the fire.

"I won't stand by and see it done, Fagin," she cried.

"You've got the boy and what more do you want? Leave him alone."

"Keep quiet!" shouted Bill Sikes.

"Women are a great trouble," said Fagin, "but we need them for our work. Charley, take Oliver to bed."

"I suppose he had better not wear his best clothes tomorrow, had he?" asked Charley Bates with a smile.

"Certainly not," said Fagin, returning the smile.

Bates led Oliver into the next room. He gave him a dirty old suit and took all his new clothes away from him.

Then, shutting the door behind him, he left Oliver alone in the dark.

Fagin kept Oliver shut up in the house for nearly a week. He told him terrible stories of boys who had run away from him and how he caused them to be hanged. He described their deaths, and said that he hoped it would never be necessary to make Oliver suffer a death like that.

Oliver was filled with fear as he listened to Fagin's words.

One cold wet night Fagin left the house. He went down the dark street and knocked at the door of another house, as old and dirty as his own.

"Who's there?" said a man's voice.

"Only me, Bill, only me, my dear."

"Come in," said Sikes.

"It's about this house at Chertsey," said Fagin, rubbing his hands. "When are we going to steal the silver from it? Such silver, my dear, such silver! When is it to be done, Bill?"

"We can't do it as we planned," said Bill. "Toby Crackit has been staying near the place for over two weeks now,

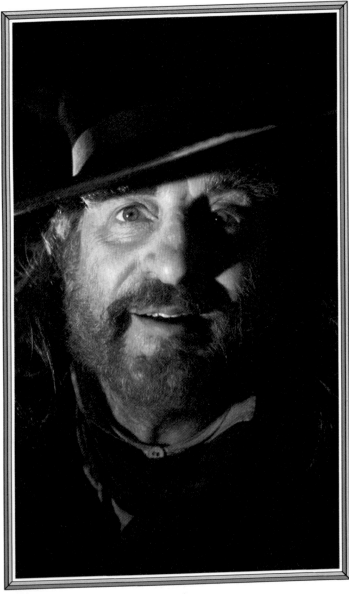

Fagin

and he can't get any of the servants to help him."

"Do you mean to tell me, Bill, that neither of the menservants can be won over to our side?"

"Yes, I do mean to tell you so," answered Sikes. "The old lady who owns the house has had those two menservants for over twenty years. If you gave them five hundred pounds they wouldn't help you. Will you give me fifty pounds extra if the work is done from the outside?"

"Yes," said Fagin.

"Then we can do it as soon as you like," said Sikes. "Toby and I climbed into the garden the night before last. We looked at all the doors and windows. The house is shut up at night like a prison. But there's one small window we can open. We need a boy to get through this window, and he mustn't be a big one."

"Oliver is the boy for you, my dear," said Fagin. "It's time he began to work for his bread, and the other boys are all too big."

Chapter 9
Bill Sikes

When Oliver awoke in the morning he was surprised to find that a new pair of shoes had been placed by his bed.

He was pleased, but his pleasure soon went when Fagin told him that he was to be taken to see Bill Sikes that night.

"To . . . to stay there, sir?" he asked in an anxious voice.

"No, no, my dear. We shouldn't like to lose you. Don't be afraid, Oliver. You shall come back to us again."

"Why am I going?" said Oliver.

"Wait till Bill tells you," said Fagin. "Be careful, Oliver. Bill Sikes is a rough man and thinks nothing of blood when he is angry. Do what he tells you. Good night." And Fagin left the room.

Oliver was terribly afraid. Falling on his knees he prayed to God to save him.

Nancy came in. She turned very white when she saw Oliver saying his prayers. She covered her face with her hands.

"Nancy!" cried Oliver. "What is it?"

"Nothing," said Nancy. "Now, dear, are you ready? You must come with me to Bill. You must be good and quiet. If you are not, you will only do harm to yourself – and me too. Give me your hand."

"So you've got the boy," said Sikes when Nancy returned. "Did he come quietly?"

"Like a lamb," said Nancy.

"I'm glad to hear it," said Sikes. "Come here, boy, and let me talk to you."

He pulled off Oliver's cap and threw it in a corner.

"Now, do you know what this is?" he asked, taking up a pistol which lay on the table.

"Yes, sir," said Oliver.

Sikes loaded the pistol with great care.

"Now it's loaded," he said when he had finished.

"Yes, I see it is, sir," said Oliver.

"Well," said Sykes, pressing the pistol against Oliver's head. "If you speak a word when you're outside, except when I speak to you, you'll be shot in the head at once. Do you hear?"

Sikes and the boy hastened through the city. The day broke as they reached the country roads. In the afternoon they came to an old inn and Sikes ordered some dinner by the kitchen fire.

They continued their journey. The night was very cold. Not a word was spoken. They walked on and on across the fields until they saw the lights of a town not far away.

They came to a bridge and Sikes turned suddenly. He left the path and went down to an old ruined house. No light could be seen. Sikes opened the door and they went inside.

"Hello!" cried a loud voice as soon as they were inside.

"Don't make such a noise," said Sikes, closing the door. "Show a light, Toby."

A man appeared, holding a candle in his hand. He had red hair and big boots and some large rings on his dirty fingers.

"I'm glad to see you, Bill," said Toby Crackit. "Is this the boy?"

"One of Fagin's," said Sikes. "Oliver Twist. Take his other hand, Toby, and off we go."

The two thieves went out with Oliver between them. It

was very dark and cold.

They went quickly through the town. After walking for about a quarter of a mile they stopped in front of a house with a wall all round it. Toby Crackit quickly climbed to the top of the wall.

"The boy next," he said. "Lift him up. I'll hold him."

Before Oliver had time to look round Sikes had caught him under the arms. In three or four seconds he and Toby were lying on the grass on the other side. Sikes followed at once. They walked towards the house.

Now, for the first time, Oliver, nearly mad with fear and terror, saw that they were planning to enter the house – to steal and perhaps to murder. He cried out and fell to his knees.

"Get up!" said Sikes in anger, drawing the pistol from his pocket. "Get up or I'll shoot you through the head."

"Oh, please let me go," cried Oliver. "Let me run away and die in the fields. Oh, have mercy on me and do not make me steal!"

Sikes put the pistol to Oliver's head. But Toby took it from him and put his hand over the boy's mouth.

"Quiet!" he whispered. "Don't shoot here. If the boy says another word I'll hit him on the head. That makes no noise and is just as good."

He and Sikes took Oliver to the back of the house. There was a small window there which Sikes was able to open. It was very small but just large enough to allow a boy of Oliver's size to enter.

"Now listen," whispered Sikes to Oliver, taking a lamp from his pocket and lighting it. "I'm going to put you through there. Take this light, go up the steps and along the little hall to the door. Open it and let us in."

Toby stood under the window with his hands on his knees to make a step of his back. Sikes stood on his back and put Oliver through the window with his feet first.

"Take this lamp," he said. "Can you see the stairs?"

"Yes," whispered Oliver, more dead than alive.

Sikes pointed to the door.

"If you don't open it, I shall shoot you at once." he said. "Now go."

Oliver had decided that, even if he died, he would make one attempt to go upstairs from the hall and wake the family. With this idea in his mind he took one step forward.

"Come back!" cried Sikes aloud. "Back! Back!"

Frightened by this loud cry. Oliver let his lamp fall.

A light appeared. He saw two men at the top of the stairs. There was another cry, a loud noise, a sudden light and smoke – and Oliver fell back. He was shot.

Sikes seized Oliver by the neck before the smoke had cleared away. He fired his own pistol after the men, who were already running away. He pulled Oliver quickly through the window.

"Give me a coat, Toby," he said. "They've hit him. Quick! There's so much blood coming from him."

Then came the noise of a bell ringing. Men were shouting. Oliver felt himself being carried quickly over the ground. Then a cold feeling came into his heart and he saw and heard no more.

Sikes rested the body of Oliver Twist across his knee. Then he shouted to Toby Crackit, "Come back and help me carry the boy. Come on!"

Toby came slowly across the field.

"Quicker!" cried Sikes.

At this moment Sikes heard a noise. Men were already climbing over the gate into the field. There were dogs with them too.

"They're after us!" cried Toby. "Drop the boy and run!"

Toby disappeared quickly, and Sikes, throwing a coat over Oliver, ran out of the other end of the field and disappeared too.

Two men came running to the middle of the field. They were the two menservants from the big house. They looked round.

"I can't see them," said the first man. "I think we should go home now."

"Yes, Mr Giles," said the other man, whose face was very white.

"You are afraid, Brittles," said the first man, whose face was even whiter.

"We're both afraid. It's only natural," said the man called Brittles.

Keeping close together, the two men went back across the fields.

The air grew colder as the day broke. The rain came down thick and fast. Still Oliver lay on the cold wet ground, without moving or feeling.

Chapter 10
Oliver is safe again

At last Oliver awoke with a cry of pain. His left arm, covered in blood, hung heavy at his side. He could not lift it. He was so weak that he could hardly sit up. He cried with the pain.

At last he got to his feet and tried to walk.

He reached a road and saw a house near it. "Perhaps the people in that house will have pity on me," he thought. "And if they don't it will be better to die near people than in the open fields."

He pushed open the garden gate, and went slowly across the grass. The pain grew worse. He climbed the steps, knocked at the door and then fell down, almost dead with pain and fear.

At this time Mr Giles, Brittles and the other servants of the big house were having some early morning tea in the kitchen. Mr Giles was telling the servants what had happened in the night.

Suddenly there was a noise outside. The cook gave a cry of alarm.

"What was that noise at the door?"

"It was a knock," said Mr Giles. "Open the door, somebody."

Nobody moved.

"It seems a strange sort of thing, a knock coming at this hour of the morning," said Mr Giles. "Open the door, Brittles. We'll all stand near you."

They advanced slowly towards the door. Brittles opened it and all they saw was poor little Oliver Twist.

"A boy!" cried Mr Giles. He seized Oliver by one leg and one arm and pulled him into the hall.

"Here he is!" he shouted up the stairs. "Here's one of the thieves, madam! Here he is! I shot him, madam."

"Giles!" came a sweet voice from a young lady at the top of the stairs.

"I'm here, miss," cried Mr Giles. "Don't be afraid, miss. I've got one of the thieves here, miss."

"Quiet!" said the young lady. "Is the poor man hurt?"

"He looks as if he was dying," shouted Brittles. "Wouldn't you like to come down and look at him, miss?"

"Do be quiet, there's a good man," said the young lady. "Wait quietly for just one moment while I speak to my aunt, and ask her what to do."

She went away and soon returned and said, "Carry the thief to Mr Giles's room. Brittles must take a horse and go to the town for the doctor."

In a pleasant and comfortable room two ladies sat at the breakfast table. Mr Giles, in a black suit, was serving them from a table at the side. One of the ladies was old; the other was not yet seventeen. She was a very beautiful girl with blue eyes and a sweet smile. Her name was Rose Maylie and the old lady was her aunt, Mrs Maylie.

A carriage stopped outside the gate. A fat gentleman jumped out of it, ran into the house and burst into the room.

"I never heard of such a thing!" he cried as he shook hands with the ladies. "My dear Mrs Maylie – in the silence of the night – and you too, Miss Rose. I never heard of such a thing! You might be dead with fright!"

"We are all right, Dr Losberne," said Rose, "but there is a poor man upstairs, that my aunt wishes you to see."

"So Brittles told me," said Dr Losberne. "You shot him, Giles? Where is he? Show me the way."

The doctor stayed in Mr Giles's room for a long time – much longer than he or the ladies had expected. He stayed there for over an hour. His bag was brought up from the carriage. A bedroom bell was rung very often and the servants ran up and down the stairs all the time.

At last Dr Losberne returned to the two ladies.

"This is a very strange thing, Mrs Maylie," he said.

"The thief is not in danger, I hope?" said the old lady.

"No," replied the doctor. "Have you seen this thief?"

"No," said the old lady.

"Nor heard anything about him?"

"No."

"I was going to tell you about him when the doctor came in, madam," said Mr Giles. The truth was that he felt rather ashamed to say that he had shot a small boy.

"Rose wished to see the man," said Mrs Maylie, "but I wouldn't allow it."

"There is nothing to be afraid of," said the doctor. "He is quiet and comfortable now. Will you both come and see him while I am here?"

The doctor led the way upstairs.

"Now," he said, as he opened the door, "let us hear what you think of him."

He drew back the curtains of the bed. There, instead of the evil creature they had expected to see, lay a child.

They looked at him in silence. Then the younger lady bent over him. As she did so her tears fell upon his face. Oliver moved, and smiled in his sleep.

"What can this mean?" said the older lady. "This poor child can never have been a thief."

"Who can say?" answered the doctor. "Bad things often live in a beautiful house. Evil, like death, can be found among the young as well as the old."

"But at so early an age!" cried Rose. "How young he is! He may never have known a mother's love or the joy of a comfortable home. Oh, aunt, dear aunt, have pity on him! Do not let them take this sick child to prison!"

"My dear love," said the old lady, "of course not!"

Hour after hour passed. Oliver was still in a heavy sleep. It was evening before Dr Losberne told the ladies that Oliver was awake and able to talk to them.

Their talk was a long one. Oliver told them the story of his life, and was often forced to stop, because of the pain and his weak condition. It was sad to hear the low voice of a sick child, telling of all the evil things he had suffered and of the terrible things which hard men had done to him.

But there were gentle hands and loving smiles to help him. He felt calm and happy and could have died in perfect peace.

Oliver grew better.

It was a completely new life for him. He went for walks with Mrs Maylie and Rose. He listened while they talked of books, and sometimes sat near them to listen while Rose read aloud. He listened too when Rose played the piano in the evenings and sang in her sweet and gentle voice.

He helped in the garden and he worked at his lessons too. He fed Mrs Maylie's birds and sometimes he got up at six o'clock in the morning to pick flowers to put on the breakfast table.

Three months passed away – months of peace and beauty. Oliver was really happy; the ladies looked after him so well and he loved them with all his heart.

Chapter 11
The mysterious stranger

Spring passed quickly and summer came.

One beautiful night Oliver and the two ladies took a longer walk than usual. When they returned Rose sat down at the piano. After playing for a little time her hands suddenly began to shake. Her face was very white.

"Rose, my love!" cried Mrs Maylie. "What is this? What is the matter?"

"Nothing, aunt, nothing," said Rose. "I am rather tired. That's all. I shall go to bed now and be better tomorrow."

When morning came, Rose was worse. It was clear that she was suffering from a serious illness. Mrs Maylie's grief was terrible.

"We must send for Dr Losberne at once, Oliver," she said. "I have written a letter to him. It must be carried to the inn. From there someone will ride at once with it to Dr Losberne at Chertsey. Will you take it to the inn for me?"

Oliver ran off at once across the fields with the letter.

He found the inn and arranged for the letter to Dr Losberne to be taken to Chertsey at once.

He was coming out of the inn when he almost fell against a tall man in a black coat.

"Curse you!" said the man in a voice of terrible anger. "Curses on your head and black death on your heart! What are you doing here?"

He advanced towards Oliver as if to hit him, and then suddenly fell to the ground.

Oliver looked for a moment at the mad man (for he thought that he must be mad) and then ran into the inn for help. Some men came and carried the strange person inside. Then Oliver ran off as fast as he could, to make up for lost time.

Late that night Dr Losberne arrived and went straight to Rose. Mrs Maylie and Oliver waited outside.

Rose had fallen into a deep sleep, from which she would awake either to get better or to die.

At last Dr Losberne came out.

"What of Rose?" cried the old lady. "Tell me at once! I can bear it. Oh, tell me, in the name of Heaven!"

"You must be calm," said the doctor. "Be calm, I pray you, my dear madam."

"Tell me in God's name! My dear child! She is dead? She is dying?"

"Thank God, no!" cried the doctor, with great feeling. "She will not die but will live for years to come."

The old lady fell upon her knees in prayer. It was almost too much happiness to bear. Oliver could not weep, or speak, or rest. He went out and picked some beautiful flowers for Rose's room.

Every day Rose grew better, but she was weak for a long time and could not leave her room. There were no more evening walks now, and Oliver spent much of the time in his own little room, working at his lessons.

One evening, after a hot summer's day, Oliver sat at his books. He had been reading for a long while and felt tired and half asleep.

Suddenly he seemed to see Fagin, pointing at him and whispering to another man, "That's the boy, sure enough. Come away."

"The boy!" the other man seemed to answer. "Could I ever mistake him?"

The man seemed to say this with such fierce anger and

Oliver works at his lessons

hatred that Oliver jumped up.

What was that, which sent the blood rushing to his heart and took away from him all power to speak or move? There – there – at the window – close to him – so close that he could have almost touched him – there stood Fagin! And beside him, white with anger or fear or both, stood the man who had met him outside the inn.

It was only a second – and they were gone. But they had seen him and he them.

He stood quite still for a moment and then, jumping from the window into the garden, called for help in a loud voice.

The servants came running. All Oliver could say was, "Fagin! Fagin!"

"Was it a man?" cried Mr Giles, taking up a heavy stick. "Which way did he go?"

"Over there!" cried Oliver.

Mr Giles ran off, Brittles followed him. Oliver ran behind, and Dr Losberne, who had been taking a short walk, joined in the hunt, but the two men could not be found.

"It must have been a dream, Oliver," said Dr Losberne.

"Oh no, indeed, sir," replied Oliver. "I saw old Fagin – I am sure of that. I saw them both as clear as I can see you now."

"Who was the other man?" asked Dr Losberne.

"The man I told you about, who was at the inn," said Oliver.

"This is very strange," said Dr Losberne. They continued to search for the two men, but without success. The next day Mr Giles was sent to all the inns for miles around to ask about the two strangers, but no one could tell him anything.

Chapter 12
Mr Bumble and the stranger

In the workhouse where Oliver was born, Mr Bumble was sitting by the fire. He was drinking his tea and reading the paper, when a man came to see him. The man was tall and dark and wore a black coat. It was the man Oliver had seen at the inn, and later outside his window with Fagin.

"Mr Bumble," said the stranger, "you are an officer of the workhouse, are you not?"

"I am now master of the workhouse," said Mr Bumble slowly and in an important voice. "Master of the workhouse, young man."

"Now please listen to me," said the stranger. "I want you to tell me something. I don't ask you to do it for nothing. Take this to begin with."

As he spoke he put two gold coins on the table. Mr Bumble took them and put them in his pocket.

"Try to remember something, Mr Bumble," said the stranger. "Let me see – twelve years ago last winter."

"It's a long time," said Mr Bumble.

"Something happened in your workhouse then," said the man. "A boy was born there, a little boy with a thin face. He was sent out to work to help make coffins. Then he ran away."

"Ah, you mean Oliver Twist!" said Mr Bumble.

"It's not of him I want to hear," said the stranger. "I wish to hear about the old woman who looked after his mother. Where is she?"

"Where is she?" said Mr Bumble. "She died last winter. She had a friend with her – another old woman from the workhouse."

"How can I find her?" asked the stranger.

"Only through me," said Mr Bumble.

"When?"

"Tomorrow."

"At nine in the evening," said the stranger, taking a piece of paper and writing an address on it. "Bring her to me at this place and in secret."

With these words he left the room. Mr Bumble looked at the paper and saw that it had no name on it. He got up and ran after the man. "What name am I to ask for?"

"Monks," answered the man and walked quickly away.

It was a hot summer evening. Mr Bumble came down to a deserted spot by the river. An old woman was with him.

"The place should be somewhere near here," said Mr Bumble, looking at the piece of paper by the light of his lamp.

"Hello!" said a voice from an old empty house just near them. "Come in, both of you."

They went in. The man in the black coat closed the door behind them.

"Now," said the stranger, addressing the old woman, "Mr Bumble tells me that you were with a certain old woman on the night she died. She told you something in secret, I believe?"

"About the mother of Oliver Twist," said the old woman. "Yes, that's right."

"What did she say?"

"How much is it worth to you?" said Mr Bumble.

"It may be worth nothing or it may be worth twenty pounds," said Monks. "Let me hear it first."

"Add five pounds to that. Give me twenty-five pounds in gold," said Mr Bumble.

Monks thought for a moment. Then he took some money from his pocket. He counted out twenty-five gold coins and gave them to Mr Bumble.

"Now," he said. "Let's hear the story."

"When old Sally died," said the old woman, "she and I were alone."

"Was there no one else near?" asked Monks. "No one who could have heard you and understood what you were saying to each other?"

"Not a soul," replied the old woman. "We were quite alone. I stood alone beside her when death came over her."

"Good," said Monks. "Go on."

"She spoke of a young girl," continued the woman, "a young girl who had brought a child – Oliver Twist – into the world some years before. Old Sally told me that the young mother had given her something before she died. She had asked her, almost with her last breath, to keep it for the child."

"And did she keep it for the boy? What did she do with it?" cried Monks.

"She kept it for herself. She never gave it to the child."

"And then?"

"She sold it to me later on, when the child had left the workhouse."

"Where is it now?" cried Monks.

"Here," said the woman. She threw a small bag on to the table. Monks tore it open. It contained a little gold ornament, in which there were two pieces of hair, and a plain gold wedding ring.

"The ring has the word 'Agnes' inside it," said the old woman. "That was the name of the child's mother."

"And this is all?" said Monks, looking again at the two small objects.

"All," replied the woman.

"Good," said Monks. "Now come with me and I will show you what I am going to do with these two orna- ments."

He led them down to the river.

"There!" said Monks, throwing the bag into the river. "That is the end of that! And you two will keep quiet about all this?"

"You may depend on us, Mr Monks," said Mr Bumble, bowing.

Chapter 13
Nancy learns a secret

Bill Sikes lay on his bed, covered by his coat. He had been ill for several weeks. A young woman sat near the window. She looked so white and thin that it was difficult to see that she was Nancy.

The door opened and Fagin came into the room.

"Now listen to me, Bill," said Fagin. "We have got to get Oliver back. He's worth a lot of money to me, Bill."

"How can you get him back?" said Bill.

"He's staying with Miss Maylie and her aunt. And I think we have a chance now, Bill. They have come to London from the country and they're staying at a hotel near Hyde Park. We'll make another attempt to get Oliver back. Nancy will help us again. Why, Nancy, how white you look!"

"White?" said the girl, covering her eyes with her hands.

"Quite terrible. What have you been doing to yourself?"

"Nothing that I know of, except sitting in this room for weeks and weeks," was the answer.

"Well, you can go out now," said Sikes. "I need some money and you can go back with Fagin to his house and get it for me."

Fagin was not very pleased, but in the end he agreed and left for home, followed by Nancy.

"Now," said Fagin when they reached his room. "I'll go and get you the money, Nancy."

They heard the sound of a man's voice on the stairs.

"It's the man I was expecting to see," whispered Fagin. "Not a word about the money while he's here, Nancy! He won't stop long."

Fagin took the candle to the door. A man in a black coat stood there. It was Monks. He drew back when he saw Nancy.

"Only one of my young people," said Fagin. "Don't move, Nancy."

Monks came in.

"Any news?" asked Fagin.

"Yes," said Monks with a smile. "I have been quick enough this time. Let me have a word with you."

Fagin led the way to another room. Nancy quickly took off her shoes, followed them and stood quietly near the door. She listened to all that they said.

Chapter 14
A visit to Rose Maylie

The next day Bill Sikes felt a little better and Nancy went out to buy food and drink with the money Fagin had provided.

Sikes drank a great deal.

Nancy watched Sikes as he drank. At last he fell back and lay in a deep and heavy sleep.

"Ah!" whispered Nancy as she rose. "The drink has made him sleep. I must go now or I may be too late."

She put on her hat and looked round in fear, as if she expected every moment to feel Sikes's heavy hand on her shoulder. She closed the door without a sound and was soon hurrying along through the busy London streets.

As the clock struck ten she entered the hall of a quiet family hotel near Hyde Park.

"Now, what do you want here?" asked one of the servants. He saw that she was white and thin and wearing old clothes.

"I want to see a lady who is staying here – Miss Maylie. Tell her that a young woman wishes to speak to her alone," said Nancy, "and it's very important."

The servant went up the stairs. Soon he returned and asked Nancy to follow him. He led her to a small room. Rose Maylie was there.

"I am the person you wanted to see," said Rose in a sweet voice. "Tell me why you have come."

The kind voice and the gentle manner took Nancy by surprise. She burst into tears.

"Oh, lady, lady!" she said. "If there were more like you

in the world there would be fewer like me!"

"Sit down," said Rose. "If you are in trouble I shall be glad to help you. Please sit down."

"Heaven bless you for being so kind," said Nancy. "I have come from people who would murder me if they knew that I was here. But I want to tell you something that I have heard. Do you know a man called Monks?"

"No," said Rose.

"He knows you, and knows you are here," said Nancy. "That is how I found this hotel."

"I never heard the name," said Rose.

"Then perhaps he has some other name," said Nancy. "I thought of that before. Last night I heard him talking to Fagin. They know that Oliver is here and they are planning to catch him again. Monks intends to pay Fagin to get Oliver back and turn him into a thief again."

"But why?" asked Rose.

"I cannot quite understand," said Nancy, "but Monks wants Fagin to turn Oliver into a thief again, so that he will lose his life. Monks said, 'That will be the end of my young brother, Oliver.'"

"His brother!" cried Rose.

"Those were his words, lady," said Nancy, "and now it is growing late and I must get back."

"Don't go," said Rose. "Stay here. You will be safe with me. Why don't we tell the police?"

"I must go back," said Nancy.

"But what am I to do?" said Rose.

"You must tell this story to some kind gentleman who will advise you what to do," said Nancy. "Oliver must be saved: that is all."

"But where can I find you again if it is necessary?" asked Rose.

"Will you promise me that you will keep my secret and come alone, or with the only other person who knows it?"

"I promise," said Rose.

"Then, if I am alive," said Nancy, "I will walk on London Bridge every Sunday night from eleven until the clock strikes twelve. And now goodbye, dear lady."

"Stay another moment," said Rose. "Why must you return to those thieves when I can save you? Will you not stay – or at least take some money so that you can lead an honest life in future? I wish to help you."

"Not a penny," said Nancy, bursting into tears. "You could help me best if you could take my life at once. I am worth nothing. God bless you, sweet lady."

Chapter 15
Old friends meet

Oliver wanted to see Mr Brownlow again, now that they were staying in London. He had told the two ladies how good and kind Mr Brownlow was, and how well he and Mrs Bedwin had looked after him.

Rose decided to visit Mr Brownlow and to tell him Nancy's secret. She went with Oliver. When they arrived at Mr Brownlow's house, she asked to see Mr Brownlow on very important business.

She left Oliver in the carriage with Mr Giles and followed the servant into an upper room. There she met an old gentleman who looked very kind. Sitting near him was another old gentleman who did not look so kind.

"Mr Brownlow, sir?" asked Rose, looking from one gentleman to the other.

"That is my name," said the one with the kind face. "This is my friend, Mr Grimwig. Grimwig, will you leave us for a few minutes?"

Rose remembered what Oliver had told her about Mr Grimwig.

She said, "I think Mr Grimwig knows the business about which I wish to speak." Mr Grimwig bowed.

"I shall surprise you very much," said Rose, "but you were once very kind to a very dear young friend of mine. I'm sure that you will be interested to hear about him again. His name is Oliver Twist."

"Indeed!" said Mr Brownlow. Both he and Mr Grimwig looked very surprised.

"A bad boy!" said Mr Grimwig. "I'll eat my head if he's not a bad boy!"   .

"He is a good boy," said Rose quickly. "He has a fine nature and a warm heart."

"Tell us what you know about this poor child," said Mr Brownlow. "We are very interested in him."

Rose told them all that had happened to Oliver. She told them too that Oliver's only sorrow was that he could not see his dear old friend, Mr Brownlow.

"Thank God!" said the old gentleman. "This is great happiness to me, great happiness. But, Miss Maylie, you have not told us where he is now. Why have you not brought him with you?"

"He is waiting in the carriage at the door," said Rose.

"At the door!" cried Mr Brownlow. He hurried out of the room and down the stairs without another word.

When he had gone Mr Grimwig rose from his chair and walked up and down the room. Then, stopping suddenly, he kissed Rose.

"Don't be afraid," he said, as the young lady rose in some alarm. "I'm old enough to be your grandfather. You're a sweet girl. I like you. Ah! Here they are!"

He returned quickly to his chair as Mr Brownlow came in with Oliver. Mrs Bedwin came too and Oliver sprang into her arms.

While Oliver and the old lady were talking and laughing and crying and kissing, Mr Brownlow led Rose into another room. There he heard the story of Nancy's visit to Rose.

"This is a very strange mystery," said Mr Brownlow, "and we shall never get to the bottom of it until we find this man, Monks."

"Only Nancy can help us there," said Rose, "and she cannot be seen until next Sunday."

Chapter 16
Midnight on London Bridge

It was Sunday night. The church clock struck the hour. Sikes and Fagin were talking but they stopped to listen. Nancy looked up and listened too. Eleven.

"A good night for business," said Sikes. "Hello, Nancy, where are you going at this time of night?"

"I'm not well," said Nancy. 'I want a breath of air."

"Then you won't have it." Sikes shut the door.

"Let me go, Bill!" cried Nancy, kneeling on the floor.

Sikes pulled her to her feet and threw her into a chair. She fought and cried until the clock struck twelve. Then she became quiet.

Fagin thought: "Nancy is tired of Bill. Perhaps I can get her to work for me against him. Perhaps I can even get her to poison him. Women have done such things before now. I must arrange for Charley Bates to follow her and see where she goes at night."

It was Sunday night again. The church clocks struck a quarter to twelve. Two people were on London Bridge. One was Nancy, and the other was Charley Bates, hiding in the shadows.

Soon two more figures appeared – a young lady and an old gentleman.

"Come down the steps here," said Nancy. "I am afraid to speak to you on the public road."

They went down the steps.

"This is far enough," said Mr Brownlow. "You were not here last Sunday, I understand?"

"I couldn't come. I was kept back by force."

"I see," said Mr Brownlow. "Now, first we must find this man Monks and learn his secret. Then Fagin must be put in prison. Oliver can never be safe while Fagin is free. You must tell the police about Fagin."

"I won't do it! I'll never do it!" cried Nancy. "Fagin is a devil – he has been worse than a devil to me – but I'll never do it!"

"Tell me why," said Mr Brownlow.

"If Fagin is taken by the police, Bill Sikes will be taken too – and I love him," said Nancy.

"Then," said Mr Brownlow, "put Monks in our hands and we will do nothing to Fagin without your permission. Tell us all you know about Monks."

Nancy began to describe him.

"He is tall and dark, with wild eyes. I think that he is young. About twenty-eight. When he walks he looks over his shoulder, first to one side and then to the other. He wears black clothes. On his neck there is——"

"A broad red mark like a burn?" cried Mr Brownlow.

"What's this?" said Nancy. "Do you know him?"

"I think I do," said Mr Brownlow. "We shall see. It may not be the same person."

He held out his hand to give Nancy some money.

"I have not done this for money," she said. "I have done it for Oliver and for the sweet lady."

"Please take the money," said Rose. "It may help you in an hour of need and trouble."

"God bless you," said Nancy. "Now I must go. Good night, good night."

She left them. Rose and Mr Brownlow went slowly up the steps of the bridge. Charley Bates had disappeared from the shadows. He was running towards Fagin's house as fast as his legs could carry him.

Chapter 17
Nancy is murdered

It was nearly two hours before sunrise. Fagin sat waiting in his room. His face was white and his eyes were red.

Charley Bates lay on the floor, fast asleep. The old man looked at him from time to time.

His thoughts were terrible ones: hatred of Nancy, who had dared to talk to strangers, anger at the failure of his plans, fear of ruin and prison and death.

He sat without moving until he heard a footstep.

"At last!" he whispered. "At last!"

He opened the door and came back into the room with Bill Sikes. Sikes carried a box, which he put on the table.

"There!" he said. "Take that. It's been trouble enough to get it. I thought I should have been here three hours ago. The police have got Dawkins. He's in prison now."

Fagin took the box and sat down again without speaking.

"What's the matter?" cried Sikes. "Why are you looking at me like that?"

Fagin looked hard at Bill. Then he turned to the sleeping boy and woke him.

"Poor Charley," said Fagin. "He's tired – tired with watching her so long – watching her, Bill."

"What do you mean?" asked Sikes.

Fagin made no answer. Charley Bates sat up and rubbed his eyes.

"Tell me what you told me before, Charley, once again – just for him to hear," said Fagin, pointing to Sikes. "About Nancy. You followed her?"

"Yes."

"To London Bridge?"

"Yes."

"And there she met two people? A gentleman and a lady. She had been to see them before. They asked her to tell them about Monks. They knew where we lived and how we could best be watched. She told them everything. She did, didn't she?" cried Fagin, half mad with anger.

"That's right," said Charley.

Sikes pulled open the door, and ran out.

When he reached his home he entered his room. He shut the door and put a heavy table against it.

Nancy was lying on the bed. She had been asleep.

"Get up!" said Sikes.

"Bill! Bill!" she said. "Tell me what I have done!"

"You know what you have done, you she-devil! You were watched tonight. You were followed to London Bridge. Every word you said was heard."

"Then spare my life for the love of Heaven. That gentleman and the dear lady will help us – I know they will. They have given me money. Let us both leave this terrible place and lead better lives far away from here. It is never too late to be sorry for the past and to start a new life."

Sikes seized his pistol. But, even in his anger, he saw that, if he fired it, the shot would be heard. He held the pistol and, with all his strength, he struck the face which almost touched his own. He struck twice.

Nancy fell. She was nearly blind with blood that poured from her head. Raising herself with difficulty to her knees, she breathed one last prayer to God for mercy.

It was a terrible sight. Sikes stepped back against the wall. He shut out the sight with his hand, then he seized a heavy stick and struck her down.

Sikes strikes Nancy

Chapter 18
Sikes escapes

The sun rose over the city. It lit the room where the murdered woman lay.

Sikes washed himself and tried to rub his clothes clean, but there were spots that could not be removed, so he cut out the pieces and burned them. The floor was covered with blood. Even the dog's feet had blood on them.

Then he went out, carrying the dog. He shut the door, took the key, and left the house.

He walked quickly through the city until he came to the country roads outside London. He lay down in a field and slept.

Morning and noon soon passed. Evening came and Sikes walked on, directing his steps to the north.

It was nine o'clock at night. Sikes was tired out, and the dog was hardly able to walk. He came to a village.

He saw the coach bringing the letters from London. It passed him on the road and stopped at the little village post office. As he drew nearer, Sikes could hear the guard talking to the man at the post office.

"Here's your bag of letters," said the guard.

"Is there anything new up in London?" asked the man at the post office.

"People are talking about a murder," said the guard. "A terrible murder!"

"Man or woman?"

"A woman," said the guard. "A young woman."

The coach drove off. Sikes went on walking. He began to feel a terrible fear. Every object on the road, every tree, every shadow, seemed like a ghost or a dead body. He seemed to see blood everywhere.

"I can't go on," he thought. "I can't spend another night alone in the fields. I'll go back to London. At least there'll be somebody to talk to there. And the police will never expect me to be staying in London. I'll hide there for a week and then get away to France. Fagin will help me."

He began his journey back. He went by different roads and he decided to enter the city by night.

"But what about the dog?" he thought. "The police must guess that the dog is with me."

He decided to drown the dog. He came near to a small river. Picking up a heavy stone, he tied it to his handkerchief. The dog looked up into his master's face.

Sikes went down to the edge of the river. The dog did not follow.

"Come here!" cried Sikes. "Do you hear me?"

The dog advanced, and then moved back.

"Come back here!" cried Sikes.

The dog stopped still for a moment, then turned, and ran away as fast as it could.

Sikes called and called, and then sat down and waited for it to return. But no dog appeared and at last Sikes continued his journey alone.

Chapter 19
Monks is caught

Night was falling when Mr Brownlow stepped down from his carriage and knocked at his own door. Two of his servants came, and together they helped out a second man from the carriage and took him into the house. This man was Monks.

"Now," said Mr Brownlow, as they sat down. "We have much to talk about."

"How dare you bring me here like this?" said Monks. "You are my father's oldest friend: how dare you treat me like this?"

"It is because I was your father's oldest friend that I wish to talk to you," said Mr Brownlow. "It is because of my friendship with your father, and my love for his beautiful sister, your aunt. I hoped to marry her, but she died young. It is because of these past loves that I wish to talk to you."

"What do you want with me?" said Monks.

"You have a brother," began Mr Brownlow.

"I have no brother," said Monks.

"Listen to me," said Mr Brownlow. "I know all your family history. I know of your father's unhappy marriage and how your father and mother separated. Your father was still young at the time. Later he met some new friends – a man and his beautiful daughter aged nineteen."

"What's this to me?" asked Monks.

"Your father fell in love with the daughter," continued Mr Brownlow. "Your father was then very rich. A member of the family had died and left him a lot of money. When your father died suddenly, all his money went to his separated wife, and to you, their son. Your father came to see me just before he died."

"I never heard of that," said Monks.

"He came," said Mr Brownlow, "and he left with me, among some other things, a picture of this young girl whom he loved. He asked me to take care of it for him. He was going to take the young girl with him and go to another country. And then – he died."

Mr Brownlow stopped for a moment.

"I went to see the young girl after his death," he said, "but she had disappeared. I never saw her again. Later her child was born in the workhouse. That child had the same father as you did. He is your half-brother – Oliver Twist. I did not know this until chance brought Oliver into my house."

"What?" cried Monks.

"Yes," said Mr Brownlow. "Oliver stayed with me for a time. I did not know who he was then, but I saw how like the picture he was. I need not tell you that he was taken away from me."

"I know nothing about that!" cried Monks.

"We shall see," said Mr Brownlow. "Let me continue. I lost the boy and could not find him. As his mother was dead, I knew that you alone could help me. I tried for a long time to find you."

"And now that you have found me," said Monks, getting up, "what difference does it make? You have no proof."

"I had none," said Mr Brownlow, "but in these past few weeks I have learned it all. You have a brother and you know it. Your father left a will which your mother destroyed. This will mentioned the future birth of a child and money to be given to this child."

"Never!" shouted Monks.

"I know it all," said Mr Brownlow. "You have tried everything – every evil plan – to destroy Oliver. Did you not tell Fagin that everything that might help Oliver lay at the bottom of the river? Can you say that this is not true?"

Monks was silent.

"I won't tell the police," said Mr Brownlow, "but Oliver must get his share of the money. I shall give you some papers to sign. And then you may go where you please. Do you agree?"

Monks, torn by fear and hatred, walked up and down the room. He could not speak.

The door opened and Mr Grimwig came in.

"News of the murder," he said. "The man will be taken tonight they think. His dog has been seen by the police. There is a hundred pounds reward for him."

"I will give fifty more," said Mr Brownlow. "What is the news of Fagin? Where is he?"

"He has not been taken yet," said Mr Grimwig. "But he will be. They are sure of him. I am quite certain that the police will take him this week!"

Monks looked at the two men in terror.

"Mr Bumble has arrived," continued Mr Grimwig. "He is downstairs. Will you see him now?"

"Yes, in one moment," said Mr Brownlow. He turned to Monks. "Have you decided?" he said in a low voice. "Do you agree to what I said?"

"Yes, yes, I agree," said Monks. "You will keep everything secret?"

"I will," said Mr Brownlow.

Mr Grimwig led Mr Bumble into the room.

"I am very glad to see you, sir," said Mr Bumble to Mr Brownlow. "And how is our dear little Oliver? I always loved that boy like a son. Dear Oliver!"

"Now," said Mr Brownlow, pointing to Monks, "do you know this person, Mr Bumble?"

"No," said Mr Bumble.

"Are you quite sure?"

"I never saw him in all my life."

"Nor sold him anything?"

"No."

"You never saw, perhaps, a certain gold ornament and ring, which one of your old workhouse women kept?"

"All right," Mr Bumble said. "I did receive some money from this man. The ornament and the ring are somewhere where you'll never get them. What then?"

"Nothing," said Mr Brownlow, "except that you are not a trustworthy person. You are not fit to be master of the workhouse. We shall see that you lose that position."

Chapter 20
The death of Sikes

Jacob's Island was in the Thames, where the river flowed through one of the lowest, dirtiest and poorest parts of London. The old houses there were empty and without roofs; the walls were falling down.

Toby Crackit and Charley Bates were hiding in one of these old houses. They were talking in frightened voices.

"When was Fagin taken?" asked Toby.

"Just at dinner time today. I escaped up the chimney," said Charley.

"They'll hang Fagin, and Sikes too when they get him," said Toby. "I tell you, Charley, we're in real danger."

"No one will find us here," said Charley.

As they sat talking, a noise was heard on the stairs, and Sikes's dog came running into the room.

"What's the meaning of this?" said Toby. "Sikes isn't coming here, is he? I ... I hope not."

Suddenly there was a knock at the door below. Toby ran to the window and looked out. His white face was enough to tell Bates who it was.

"We must let him in," said Charley, taking up a candle.

Sikes came in. His face looked old and tired; he had a beard of three days' growth.

"The paper tonight says that Fagin has been taken. Is it true?"

"True," said Charley.

They were silent again.

"Curse you both!" said Sikes, passing his hand over his face. "Have you nothing to say to me?"

"You devil!" shouted Charley Bates. "I'm not afraid of

you! Toby may let you stay here, but I'm not going to help you."

Sikes threw him to the floor. His knee was on Charley's neck when a loud knocking was heard. There were lights outside, and voices.

"Open this door in the name of the law!"

"They're here! They've found us!" whispered Toby, white with terror.

The voices outside grew louder. Some of the crowd were trying to climb the wall. Some cried out for ladders, others said they would set the house on fire.

"The tide!" cried Sikes. "The tide is out. Give me a rope, Toby, a long rope. The people are all at the front of the house. I'll drop down at the back."

Toby gave him a rope. He went to the top of the house. He climbed to the edge of the roof and looked over.

The water was out and the bed of the river was just one stretch of mud.

The crowd outside shouted as Sikes appeared on the roof. At the same time he heard noises inside the house. People were entering.

Sikes tied one end of the rope round the chimney. He tied the other end round himself.

"I can let myself down nearly to the ground," he thought, "and then I can cut the rope and drop. I've got my knife ready in my hand."

At that moment he looked behind him on the roof, threw his arms above his head and gave a shout of terror.

"Those eyes again!" he cried. "I can still see her eyes!"

He fell back and dropped from the roof. The rope slipped round his neck. He fell for ten metres, and then there was a sudden stop. There he hung and swung against the wall – dead.

The crowd shouts as Sikes appears on the roof

Chapter 21
The end of the story

Fagin sat in prison. Looking at the floor, he tried to collect his thoughts. After a while he began to remember a few words of what the judge had said to him: "To be hanged by the neck."

As it grew dark he began to think of all the men he had known who had died in this way. Some of them had died because of him.

The night passed in silence, broken only by the church clocks striking. The sound of every bell brought him the same message – Death.

Out story is nearly over. We can finish it in a few words.

After Fagin's death, Charley Bates decided that, after all, an honest life was best. He turned his back on the dark days of the past and began a new and happy life, working for a farmer.

Monks went to America; he wasted all his money there and died in prison.

Mr Brownlow took Oliver to live with him as his son. With old Mrs Bedwin, they moved to a house in the country. Their house was about a mile away from the house where Mrs Maylie and Rose lived.

Mr Giles and Brittles still stayed there as servants to Mrs Maylie. Dr Losberne went back to Chertsey, but, after a few months, he decided that the air there did not agree with him, so he moved to the village too. Mr Grimwig often came down from London to visit them all.

It was a great joy for young Oliver to have his good friends so near him.

Questions

Questions on each chapter

1 *Oliver asks for more*
   1 Where did Oliver's mother die?
   2 What food did the boys have every day?
   3 What did Oliver say to the master?
   4 How much was offered to anyone who would take Oliver?

2 *He goes out to work*
   1 What did Mr Sowerberry make?
   2 Where was Oliver's bed?
   3 What was the name of the big boy?

3 *He runs away*
   1 Who made life unpleasant for Oliver?
   2 What did Noah say about Oliver's mother?
   3 What did Oliver do to Noah?
   4 When did Oliver run away?

4 *London*
   1 How far was it to London?
   2 What town did Oliver reach on the seventh morning?
   3 What was the strange boy's name?
   4 What things were hanging on the line?

5 *Fagin*
   1 What was in Fagin's box?
   2 What was the name of the boy with Jack Dawkins?
   3 What had Dawkins got?
   4 What were the names of the two girls?

6 *Oliver among the thieves*
   1 What was the old gentleman doing at the bookshop?
   2 What did Dawkins do to him?

3 What was the old gentleman's name?
4 Where did he take Oliver?

7 *A better home*
   1 Who was Mrs Bedwin?
   2 Mr Brownlow pointed at two things. What were they?
   3 Who was Mr Grimwig?
   4 What did Oliver have when he left the house?

8 *Back among the thieves*
   1 Who was the young woman?
   2 Two people took Oliver to Fagin's house. Who were they?
   3 What did Bill Sikes take from Fagin?
   4 Why did Nancy throw Fagin's stick in the fire?

9 *Bill Sikes*
   1 Who saw Oliver saying his prayers?
   2 Describe Toby Crackit.
   3 Who took the pistol away from Sikes?
   4 Who were Mr Giles and Brittles?

10 *Oliver is safe again*
   1 Where was Oliver's wound?
   2 Who were having tea in the kitchen?
   3 How old was Rose Maylie?
   4 What was the name of the doctor?

11 *The mysterious stranger*
   1 Where did Oliver run to?
   2 What did the man in the black coat say?
   3 What did Oliver get for Rose's room?
   4 Who were at Oliver's window?

12 *Mr Bumble and the stranger*
   1 Who came to see Mr Bumble?
   2 What was the stranger's name?
   3 What did the small bag contain?
   4 Where did Monks throw the bag?

13 *Nancy learns a secret*
   1 How long had Bill Sikes been ill?
   2 Why did Sikes tell Nancy to go to Fagin's house?
   3 What did Nancy listen to at the door?

14 *A visit to Rose Maylie*
   1 Where did Nancy go?
   2 What name had Rose never heard?
   3 Who must Rose tell this story to?
   4 When will Nancy walk on London Bridge?

15 *Old friends meet*
   1 Who did Rose decide to visit?
   2 Where was Oliver waiting?
   3 Who hurried out of the room?
   4 What did Mr Grimwig do to Rose?
   5 Whose arms did Oliver spring into?

16 *Midnight on London Bridge*
   1 Who prevented Nancy from going to London Bridge?
   2 What four people were on London Bridge the following Sunday?
   3 Where did Mr Brownlow listen to Nancy?
   4 Who heard Nancy and Mr Brownlow talking?

17 *Nancy is murdered*
   1 Where was Dawkins?
   2 Who did Charley tell Sikes about?
   3 Where did Sikes run?
   4 Sikes hit Nancy with two things. What were they?

18 *Sikes escapes*
   1 Where did Sikes sleep?
   2 What stopped at the village post office?
   3 Where would the police not expect to find Sikes?
   4 What did Sikes decide to do to his dog?

19 *Monks is caught*
   1 Who received Monks's father's money?
   2 What did Monks's father leave with Mr Brownlow?
   3 What had the police seen?
   4 What will happen to Mr Bumble?

20 *The death of Sikes*
   1 Who were hiding on Jacob's Island?
   2 What did Sikes do to Charley?
   3 What did Toby give Sikes?
   4 What did Sikes want to do?

21 The end of the story
    1 What was going to happen to Fagin?
    2 What message did the sound of every bell bring?
    3 What happened to Charley Bates?
    4 Where did Monks go?
    5 Who moved out of London with Mr Brownlow?
    6 Who came down from London to visit them?

Questions on the whole story

These are harder questions. Read the Introduction, and think hard about the questions before you answer them. Some of them ask for your opinion, and there is no fixed answer.

1 What was wrong with the workhouse that Dickens describes?

2 Are there still gangs like Fagin's anywhere in the world?

3 What "marks" do you think Oliver took out of handkerchiefs?

4 What did Bill Sikes do for a living?

5 Why was Oliver's face so much like the face in the picture in Mr Brownlow's house?

6 What do you think of Mr Grimwig? Pages 26 and 55 may help you here.

7 How did the women in the story treat Oliver Twist?
(a) Mrs Sowerberry (b) Nancy (c) Mrs Bedwin (d) Mrs Maylie and Rose

8 Monks:
What relation was he to Oliver?
Why did he want Oliver to become a thief?
What did he do with the things that proved who Oliver was?
Why did Mr Brownlow not tell the police about Monks?
Where did he die?

9 What reason did Dickens's readers have to hate each of these?
(a) Mr Bumble (b) Fagin (c) Bill Sikes (d) Monks